EARTHMAKER'S TALES

For Kirsten

with admiration

for

good teachers!

Gretchen Will Mayo

10/21/93

NORTH AMERICAN INDIAN STORIES

Earthmaker's Tales

Retold and Illustrated by
Gretchen Will Mayo

WALKER AND COMPANY
NEW YORK

First paperback edition published in the United States of America in 1990 by the Walker
Publishing Company, Inc.

Published simultaneously in Canada by
Thomas Allen & Son Canada, Limited, Markham, Ontario.

Book design by Laurie McBarnette

Library of Congress Cataloging-in-Publication Data

Mayo, Gretchen.
Earthmaker's tales : North American Indian stories / by
Gretchen Will Mayo. — 1st pbk. ed.
p.   cm.
Includes bibliographical references.
Summary: A collection of Indian legends about such natural
phenomena as thunder and lightning, earthquakes, tornados, and
rainbows.
ISBN 0-8027-7343-5 (pbk.)
1. Indians of North America—Legends. 2. Nature—Folklore.
[1. Indians of North America—Legends. 2. Nature—Folklore.]
I. Title.
[E98.F6M34   1990]
398.26—dc20
[398.2]
[E]   90-12785
CIP

Printed in the United States of America

Originally published in hardcover in 1989 by the Walker Publishing Company, Inc.

2   4   6   8   10   9   7   5   3

For my mother, Julia, whose sense of adventure
is also her gift.

CONTENTS

Earth event . . . . Source tribe

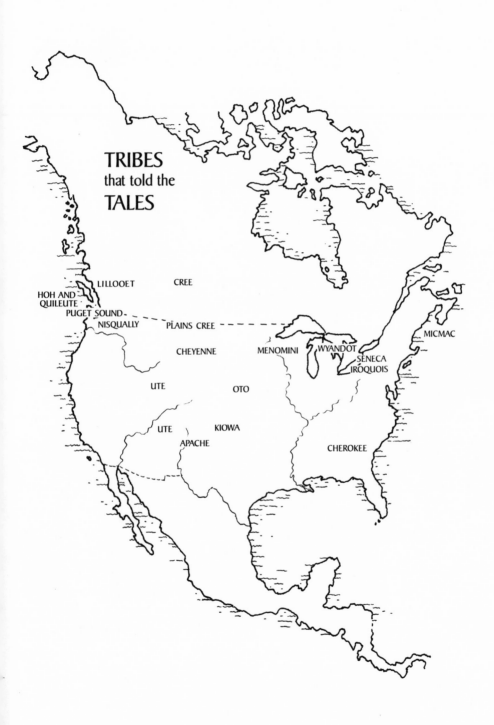

TRIBES
that told the
TALES

LILLOOET   CREE

HOH AND
QUILEUTE
PUGET SOUND
NISQUALLY   PLAINS CREE

                                                              MICMAC

                  CHEYENNE   MENOMINI   WYANDOT
                                              SENECA
                                              IROQUOIS

UTE   OTO

UTE   KIOWA

APACHE   CHEROKEE

INTRODUCTION

BLAM! CRASH!

With a thundering roar, the avalanche hurled down on good Algoot. Boulders smashed around him. Rocks flew in the dust. But Algoot had gathered super strength from the good spirits. He dodged the crushing boulders and threw them back at the wicked Tauquitch high on the mountain top. The people rejoiced when Algoot killed the evil creature. Because they used green wood to burn Tauquitch's body, however, his angry spirit lives on.

"It is cruel Tauquitch who makes the mountains rumble and the rocks fall from the ledges," says the old Saboba Indian storyteller.

Earth events have astonished, puzzled, terrified, and tormented people since the world began.

Tornadoes roared into the camps of our ancestors. Earthquakes rattled their bones. Storm clouds threatened destruction, and rainbows signaled calm.

From the beginning, the wise ones searched for ways to explain these things. "Why did Earthmaker bring the storm?" the Winnebago asked; and, "Who has made Earthmaker angry?" Their reasoning led to stories that helped to make sense of puzzling and frightening events.

Stories also made people laugh and forget their worries. Indians, often wonderfully creative, shared and traded their tales from tribe to tribe or with people who were not Native Americans. Because early Indians had not developed a written language, it was the European missionaries and explorers who usually recorded their stories for the first time. The tales, however, were not always written exactly as they were told. On the other hand, loving a good story, Indians wove parts of some European folktales into their own. Some legends, of course, were sacred and could never be given away or changed, even to this day.

In early days, the time and setting for storytelling was very important. Rules had to be followed, although the rules varied from tribe to tribe.

Like many other tribes, the Blackfoot insisted on telling their legends after dark and in the winter time. Stories often continued far into the night, lengthened and embellished with details and colorful descriptions. The Yavapai of central Arizona considered it dangerous to tell their stories during the summer months, when spiders and snakes might hear and bite them. They waited for storytelling until autumn, when the animals began their long sleep and couldn't listen. Then they built a good fire and sat in a circle around one of the elders of the tribe, a keeper of the old stories.

Early Native Americans lived close to the land and knew its many moods and signs. They had stories for streams they crossed, blazing sunsets, and windy storms. To them, all creation was alive with spirits, and all things were connected. From this rich treasure, born and nurtured in their lives, these tales are retold with gratitude.

EARTHMAKER'S TALES

EARTHQUAKE

"There are too many new people!" cried the Wintu storyteller when the earth quaked. "Coyote Old Man is stretching and pulling the earth to make it larger."

Far eastward across the continent, the Yuchi Indians told about a mysterious creature of the underworld who shook the earth from time to time to see how much water remained on top.

The earthquake story of the Wyandots explained how the world began. The word Wyandot means, "They are islanders," an appropriate name for a tribe living in the land of the Great Lakes between lakes Huron, Michigan, and Superior. They traded furs with the French and the English, and their history was often linked with that of the Iroquois.

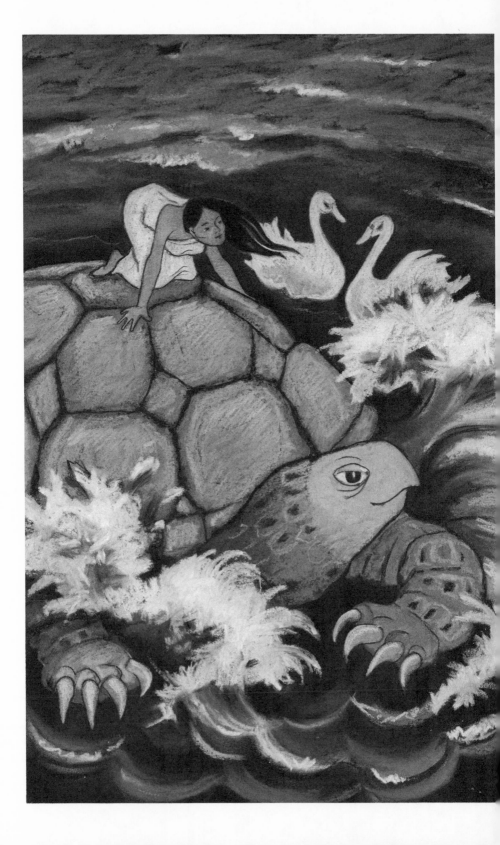

EARTH IS ON BIG TURTLE'S BACK

BACK BEFORE the world was made, Sky Woman, the beautiful daughter of Big-Chief-Above, was watching some of the people dig around a wild apple tree in the sky country. Suddenly a loud noise made the people jump back. They had broken through the floor of the sky country! The tree was sinking, making a big hole! As it dropped, the apple tree caught Sky Woman in its branches.

Falling down, down, out of the sky, the woman landed on the backs of two swans who were swimming below in the endless sea. The swans were glad to let the beautiful daughter rest on their backs after her fall, but after a while, one of them said, "This woman from the sky needs a home of her own."

So they called a council of all those living in the water.

Big Turtle had an idea. "Maybe someone can take a little mud from the tree that fell from the sky," he suggested. "Then we could make an island to float on the water."

But the tree had sunk deep into the sea. Otter, Muskrat, Beaver, and Loon all dove to find the tree but failed. Then Old Toad said that she would like to try. Old Toad was so small and ugly that everyone laughed and laughed.

3

"Quiet!" said Big Turtle. "Maybe Old Toad will do what no one else has done."

Old Toad took a deep, deep dive and was gone a long, long time. Everyone waited.

"Old Toad is too small and feeble," said Muskrat.

"Old Toad is never coming back," sighed Loon.

But little bubbles appeared on the water. Then Old Toad splashed to the surface, ready to burst, and spat out a mouthful of mud which landed right on Big Turtle's back.

Little Turtle at once began to spread the earth all around the edges of Big Turtle's shell. "Big Turtle," she said, "it looks like you have been chosen to make a home for Sky Woman!"

Big Turtle swelled with pride and the mud began to grow. When the earth became the size of a little island, Sky Woman left the swans and stepped onto Big Turtle's back, calling it her home.

Earth grew and grew until it was as large as the world is today. Sometimes Big Turtle gets a little tired holding up the earth. He moves one of his feet. He stretches the other foot. Then earth shakes and rumbles and the people shout, "Earthquake!"

FLOOD

The Utes called themselves the People of the Shining Mountains. Living in the Rocky Mountain area, they told this story about Pike's Peak and a world-wide flooding of the Colorado River.

Other Native American tribes have great flood stories too. A Chitimachan tale from southern Louisiana is like many of them. All the people except a man and a woman were destroyed by a huge flood. They were saved when they made a large earthen vessel, and a dove brought them a single grain of sand from which a new land grew.

In a Papago story, the boulders on the mountain tops are the rocky forms of people who asked the Great Spirit to save them from the pain of drowning in the great flood.

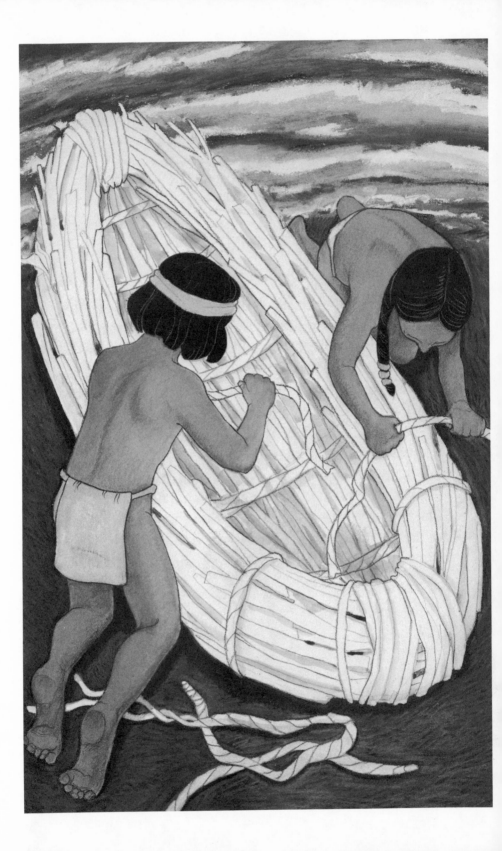

THIRSTY LIZARD ENDS THE BIG FLOOD

WHEN ALL things began, earth was called the lower world because the home of the most powerful gods was above in the heavens. The less important spirits, who directed the lower world, lived below along a great river that lay across the earth like a rope, winding in the direction of the setting sun.

To carry out their wishes, the spirits of the lower world made people. But the people made endless trouble. They argued and squabbled and fought with each other until the spirits could stand it no longer.

"Why did we make these awful people?" complained the voices of the spirits across the land. "They help a little but spoil a lot!"

The spirits of the lower world ended their misery by making the Great River grow. It grew till the waters overflowed its banks, till it overran the other rivers, till it covered all the land and all the troublesome people.

There were some things of the earth, however, that the spirits loved. So before the waters had crept to every corner, they hurried about the land collecting treasures. They gathered silver and gold and sparkling rocks and even some of

the rich brown soil to take with them to the upper world
in the sky. And they took corn, because a meal without
corn was like a day without laughter.

"No earthly treasures allowed in the sky country!" roared
the spirits of the upper world when the lesser spirits came.

Because they feared the gods, the spirits of the lower
world dropped their great loads of earth's treasures, but
secretly they hid away their corn. All the gold and silver
and shining rocks fell from the heavens, landing on earth
in a heap so huge that its peak rose above the deep waters.
And there it sat while time rolled on.

Although the spirits of the lower world had moved to
the sky country, they still kept watch over the earth. One
night, as they traveled across the sky, they saw that two
children had survived the great flood and were living on
the heap of earthly treasures.

"See how that boy and girl gather the kernels we drop!"
remarked the spirits above as they munched their ears of
corn.

"Look how they plant some of the kernels in the dark,
warm earth," they said later.

Then, after the passing of many moons, the spirits saw the boy and girl lash together corn stalks, tall and green, to make a boat.

"How clever those earth children are!" exclaimed the spirits. "How strong they have become!"

Then the spirits said to one another, "Maybe these people have earned our help. Maybe we should send them the thirsty giant."

There lived among the misty clouds a giant lizard who sipped and licked and lapped from dawn to dusk but was still always thirsty. The spirits of the lower world lead this thirsty lizard to the edge of the sky and let it dive down, down to the watery earth. With great thirsty gulps, the lizard drank and drank and drank until the heap of earthly treasures began to rise as a mountain above the sinking waters.

When Thirsty Lizard had licked the last drops of water from the land, he tried to leap high into the wet, misty clouds. But his swollen body would not rise. He fell back against the mountain of earth's treasures with a thundering crash and never moved again.

Thirsty Lizard lay there so long that his huge body turned to stone, water trickling from his scrapes and scratches. Streams bubbled from beneath the rock, tumbling down his mountainous sides to enrich the valleys below.

The people became many people. Some of them grew corn in the fertile land. some of them found the earth's treasures hidden in the mountain. They tried not to argue or squabble or fight with each other, for there was plenty for everyone. And so it was as time rolled on.

The spirits of the lower world still move across the heavens every night as groups of stars, munching their favorite food, then disappearing behind the mountains when the sun brings dawn. Sometimes the spirits are sloppy eaters. Then the kernels spill from the heavens and people below point to the sky and cry, "Look at the falling stars!"

DAYLIGHT

Many Indian legends say that the young world was always dark. Some tribal stories tell of a tricky hero who managed to light the world for the people. Sometimes Coyote was the hero. Sometimes, as in this Lillooet tale from the far Northwest, it was Raven.

In a story from the Northwest Tsimshian, the son of the Great Chief in the Sky changed the eternal darkness by wearing a mask of flaming pitch wood. He still wears it as he runs across the sky each day, bringing light to the world.

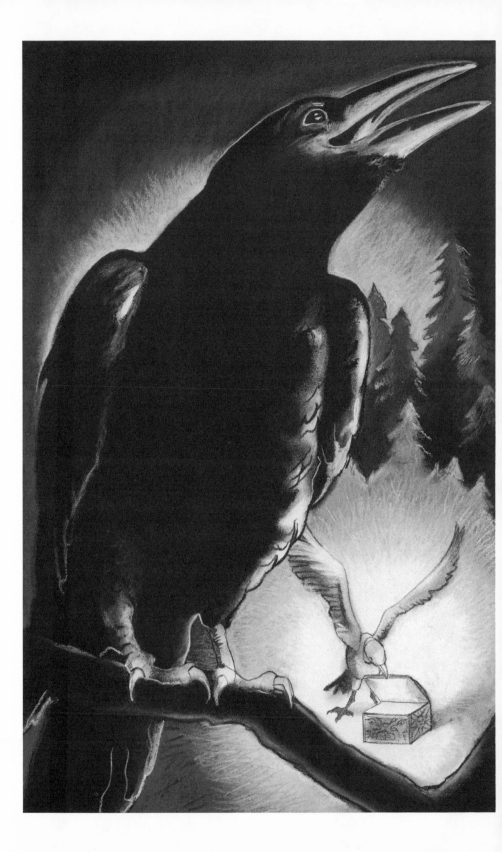

DAYLIGHT COMES AT LAST

It WAS THE time of endless night and Black Raven set out to see what he could find. Bumping through the forest, skimming past the rocks, Raven felt his way blindly through the darkness.

Suddenly a shimmer of brilliant light flashed deep among the trees. Black Raven folded his wings and crept cautiously to find out what was going on. Then, where the trees thinned to meet the water, Raven found his old friend, Sea Gull. Sea Gull was so busy fastening shut a box that he didn't notice Raven, dark as night.

"What is it you have in your box," asked the curious Raven, surprising his friend.

"Nothing much," snapped Sea Gull. But the way he hurried off with his box made Raven certain that it held a treasure.

Raven decided to stay near Sea Gull's lodge to try to find out more. Soon Raven heard Sea Gull mumbling and fumbling in the dark. Raven crept to the door of the lodge and peered in. Sea Gull was doing something with his box. He opened the lid a little crack. Suddenly the lodge was flooded with light! Raven could see each basket, every stick and every feather on Sea Gull's head. Black Raven crouched in the dark and watched Sea Gull work about his lodge without a stumble or a fumble or a bump.

"What a treasure Sea Gull has!" thought Raven. "Everyone should have this thing." But when Sea Gull was ready to sleep, Raven watched him snap down the lid of the box firmly, shutting the light back inside it, before hiding the box under his bed. "That selfish Sea Gull wants to keep his treasure all to himself," thought Raven. "Let's see what I can do to make him share it!"

Then, while Sea Gull slept soundly over his box, Raven clipped hawthorne branches from the trees around Sea Gull's lodge. Carefully, carefully, so that the long thorns wouldn't scratch him, Raven laid the branches along the path leading from Sea Gull's lodge to the water's edge. He covered the path right down to the place where Sea Gull's canoe was fastened to a stump. Then Raven untied the rope and set the canoe adrift.

"Sea Gull! Sea Gull!" shouted Raven as the canoe drifted away with the current. "Sea Gull! Your boat is floating off! Hurry!"

Sea Gull leaped from his sleep. He bumped through his doorway and bounded down the path. "OUCH! Oh! Ouch, ouch!" screeched Sea Gull. He jumped from one leg to the other right back to his house. "Raven, save my boat! My feet are full of thorns," cried Sea Gull from his doorway.

When Raven had brought back the canoe, he found Sea Gull picking the thorns from his feet.

"Let me help you," offered Raven, peering closely at Sea Gull's feet. Then, "How I wish I could see better to help my old friend," sighed Raven.

Sea Gull reached under his bed and snatched the hidden box. "Here," he moaned. "I'll give you a little light," and he opened the box a crack.

"Such big thorns!" exclaimed Raven, pulling out one, two, three. "But these little ones, I can see them hardly at all."

Groaning loudly, Sea Gull opened the box a little wider.

Raven picked and picked. "One more to go," he breathed. "Give me a little more light."

This time when Sea Gull reached for the box, Raven gave Sea Gull a little shove. The box fell open wide and all the daylight escaped. Light flooded every corner of the house. It spread outside, down the path, shimmering across the water and over the hills.

"Come back! Come back!" shouted Sea Gull to his escaping treasure. He flew out the door, racing across the hills and grasping, grasping to gather back his precious Daylight. But it was too late. Daylight was spreading across the world, coming at last to all the people.

Raven, black as night, had to listen to Sea Gull's loud complaints as long as Daylight glowed. But when Daylight traveled on to the other side of the world and night came, Sea Gull yawned and fell asleep. Then Raven, black as the night, slipped into the forest to see what else he could find.

MOUNTAINS

There are many Native American tales explaining how the mountains came to be. In some, when the soft earth was being formed, Coyote ran all over leaving his footprints and digging up the mud. In those tribes living near volcanoes, the mountains were often said to be living, growing beings who became angry and even ate people.

The Apache lived in the dry plains area just east of the high mountains. In their stories, the first people came up from the underworld and found the earth inhabited by monsters. Like most tribes, the Apache believed the sun was a being with immense power. Sun's son also had special powers, but he was more like the people and was often called to help them.

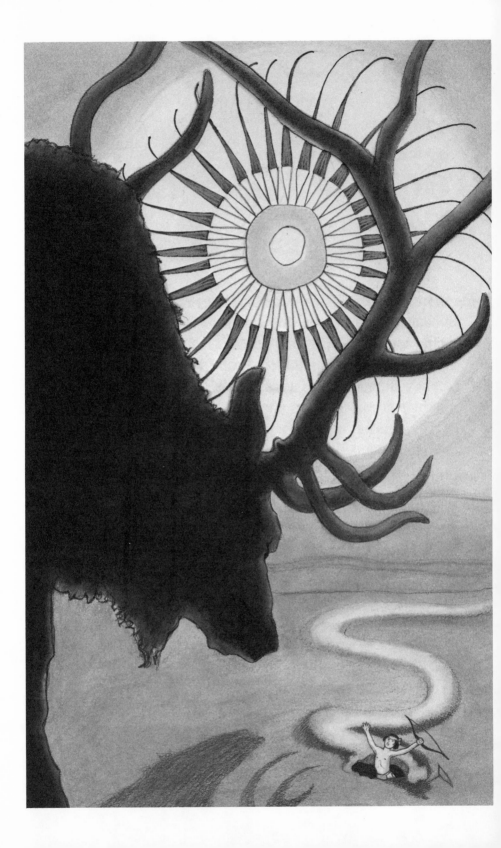

BIG ELK DIGS UP THE MOUNTAINS

IN THE earliest times, all the land on earth was flat, and all the animals were gigantic monsters. Big Elk was the most terrible of all. He sprawled across the warm dry plain and gobbled up people for snacks.

The people cried out to the gods for help, so Father Sun sent his own son to see what he could do. Son of Sun crept to Big Elk's resting place to watch from behind some tall dry grass. There were no bushes or trees on the open plain, and Son of Sun wondered how he could creep closer without being seen. As he sat and pondered, Lizard, who was sunning on a rock nearby, called out, "What are you doing here, my friend?"

"My father sent me to help the people," explained the surprised son of the sun. He told Lizard how Big Elk had been gobbling the people one-by-one. "But the plain is so flat and bare," he said. "How can I get close enough to shoot Big Elk with my arrows?"

Lizard's beady eyes blinked. "The desert is home to us lizards. We sun on the rocks and rest in the shade. There are so many of us, Elk hardly notices."

"But why doesn't he gobble you like he gobbles the people?" asked Son of Sun.

"Why do I eat flies?" answered Lizard, with a flick of his long tongue. "It's just a question of taste. Maybe if you looked like a lizard, Big Elk wouldn't want you for a snack either," suggested Lizard. He wriggled out of his coat and offered it to Son of Sun.

The son of the sun squeezed one arm into Lizard's tight coat. As he was tugging at the other, the ground beneath him heaved, and up popped Gopher, knocking Son of Sun right off his feet!

"Why were you standing right over the door to my tunnel?" huffed Gopher.

"Why did you dig your door right under my feet?" answered Son of Sun.

Then Gopher peered hard at Son of Sun. "Why on earth are you wearing Lizard's coat?" she sniffed.

The son of the sun explained why he had come to the desert plain. "If Big Elk makes a meal of me, I won't be much help to the people," he said, "so Lizard gave me his coat."

"My, my, my," sighed Gopher. "To Elk you'll just look like a tasty snack in a coat that doesn't fit. But maybe I can help. If you follow my tunnel, Big Elk will never see you."

With this, Gopher dove back into her hole. Dirt flew and the ground quivered, but soon Son of Sun could see the path of a long tunnel winding across the flat plain toward the giant elk.

Gopher was gone a long time.

Even when the burrow reached the place where Big Elk rested, Gopher did not return.

"Maybe Big Elk gobbles gophers too," thought Son of Sun mournfully. Then suddenly the ground heaved again and up popped Gopher, knocking Son of Sun right off his feet.

20

"Why do you always stand over my door?" huffed Gopher.

"Why do you always dig your door right under my feet?" answered Son of Sun.

Then Gopher peered hard at the son of the sun. "Stop asking so many questions," she sniffed. "Go after Big Elk!"

So the son of the sun plunged into Gopher's tunnel, following it far under the dry, flat plain.

Thumpa, thumpa, THUMPA, THUMPA!

A terrible pounding overhead shook the earth around him. Son of Sun looked up and saw Elk's hide thumping right over his head. This was the beating of Big Elk's giant heart! Gopher had brought him to a spot right under the monster elk.

Without wasting a moment, the son of the sun drew his bow. Four times his arrows shot above.

But to giant Big Elk, they were like the sting of four bees. The angry elk rose up on his four tall legs to see who was stinging him and he looked right down into Gopher's tunnel at the son of the sun!

"Oh, no!" yelled Son of Sun as the enraged giant plunged

his giant antler into Gopher's tunnel. The son of the sun turned in the tunnel and ran for his life.

Furious, Big Elk gouged his way along the burrowed path after Son of Sun, ploughing up mountains of dry brown earth with his sharp antlers.

Son of Sun ran and ran. When he came to the end of the tunnel, Big Elk was right behind him. But Big Black Spider was able to help the son of the sun. He lowered a tight, strong web and blocked the charging elk so that Son of Sun could get away.

By now the monster elk was so angry that he went right on ploughing up the earth, gashing and rutting from one end of the land to the other until finally he gasped his last raging breath and dropped dead.

Son of Sun thanked Big Black Spider and the people thanked Son of Sun. From that time on, the children of fearsome Big Elk were much smaller. Father Sun ruled that his elk children would eat grasses and plants rather than people. But some things remained the same. Gopher still digs tunnels. Lizard still suns on the desert rocks. And the tall mountains ploughed by Big Elk still stand high above the flat, dry plains.

WHIRLWIND

Whirlwinds, tornadoes, and cyclones inspired exciting Native American tales. In a Blackfoot story shared by many tribes, an orphan boy rescues the people who have been devoured by Windsucker, the tornado, who was said to be a giant sucker fish. The boy kills Windsucker by doing a jumping-up dance inside the monster's belly, with a knife fastened, blade upright, on his head.

The Seneca named the tornado Dagwa Noenyent and said it was a giant rolling head that could tear the largest trees from the earth.

The ancient Kiowa Indians claim that their people are the ones who made the first tornado, and that if they spoke to it, the tornado would pass without harming them. This is their story.

THE MAKING OF
WHIRLWIND

HOT SUMMER lay upon the people like a heavy moist blanket. Not a leaf moved. No whisper of a breeze lifted a strand of hair.

The people gathered around an old medicine man. "Tell us what we can do. There is hardly a breath in this hot, stuffy air," they said.

The old man sent some women to the river bank to gather red mud. When they returned he told the people to watch carefully. Then he shaped the mud into the form of an animal. It looked something like a horse, with four legs and a long tail.

"Watch me, and do what I do," said the old man to the people who were gathered around. Then the old man blew into the nostrils of the horse and it began to grow.

"Blow hard!" the old man commanded the people. They blew at the horse as hard as they could and it grew larger still until three people were needed to hold it, then ten. As they held the red mud horse, it began to stretch and twist.

"Red horse, I name you Red Wind!" called out the old man. "Now show us what you can do to cool the people."

With that, the horse tore away from the many hands that were holding it and whirled through the air, stirring it and laughing and blowing up dust.

At first the people cheered and lifted their arms to the cooling gusts. But the wind blew the feathers from their hair and the bracelets from their wrists. Red Wind twisted and jumped like a wild thing. Trees snapped as though they were twigs.

"Now look what you've done, old man!" shouted the people. "Red Wind will tear up·the earth and blow us all away!"

So the old man called out again, "Red Wind! I made you. I named you. Now I give you a home. From this time on, you will live in the sky."

Ever since then, Red Wind, the whirlwind, has lived among the black clouds. But sometimes he twists and stretches down because he likes to kick things up on earth again.

RAIN STORM

"Those lazy Cloud People don't want to work!" grumbled the Zia Indians whenever thunder and lightning came before the rain. They said the rumble of the Thunders' flapping wings and the flaming arrows shot by the Lightning People were meant to frighten the Cloud People into making rain for the parched earth.

The hero of this Seneca story about rain storms is a woman. Among the Seneca, women had great power. Chiefs and tribal council members were nominated by women, and the women removed them if they misbehaved. Women were said to prevent some wars.

The Seneca were the largest tribe in the Iroquois Confederacy. They lived in the area of northern New York State where Lake Ontario and Lake Erie come together.

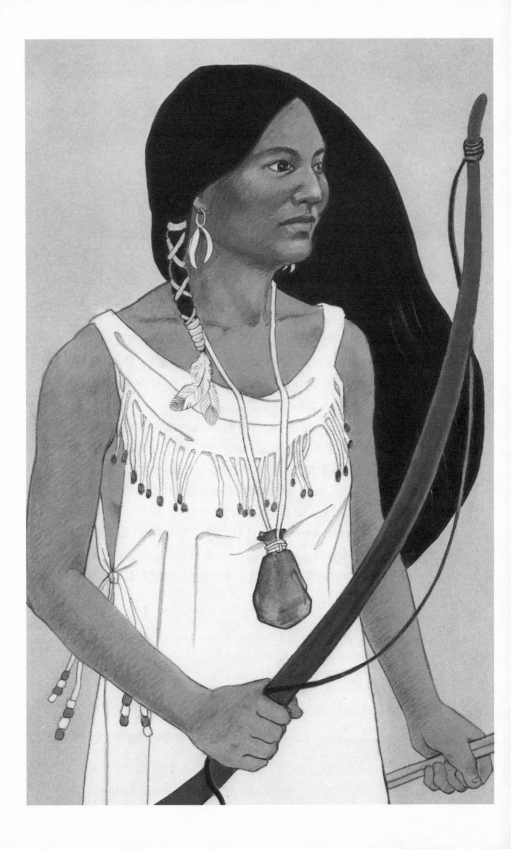

BRAVE GIRL AND THE STORM MONSTER

JIJOGWEH, the evil monster bird, made the storms and lived on the blood of humans.

The terrified people never knew when the wandering, blood-thirsty, evil bird would swoop down out of the clouds. They crept about carefully and watched the skies, but Jijogweh was as cunning as he was swift and powerful. Sweeping his gigantic wings down along the lakes and rivers, he made the waters churn and hiss until clouds boiled up to hide him. Then with one touch of his wings, the clouds turned angry black, pouring dreadful rain and slimy snakes on the poor frightened people.

There were some people who found the courage to shoot their arrows at Jijogweh when he flew at them, but none of them lived to tell of it. If his poison breath hadn't killed them first, their arrows fell back broken as Jijogweh attacked. And should even one feather fall from his wing, the blood drops turned to rock, smashing those still alive below.

One night as all the people slept, a dream message came to a strong young woman named Brave Girl. She should shape a strong bow from the wood of an ash tree, stringing it with her own long black hair. The message added that

29

if she also feathered her arrows with down from the breast of a young eagle, she could destroy the terrifying monster bird.

The young woman didn't waste time thinking of what might happen to her. Brave Girl left at dawn, climbing a high rocky cliff to an eagle's nest. When she dropped tasty bits of meat into the baby birds' open mouths, they let her pluck a handful of down. Hurrying home, the young woman made her bow and arrows just as the dream message had told her. Then she found the medicine man, who placed around her neck a pouch of sacred tobacco, asking the good spirits to help her and giving her some sacred words.

Feeling the protection of the good spirits and trusting her strong bow and arrows, the young woman waited for dark. Then she went alone to the edge of the water and crawled under some sheltering grape vines. All night she watched for the monster bird, but no living thing stirred.

"The evil one is busy somewhere else," Brave Girl thought. Suddenly, as she was gathering her things to leave, there was a terrible shriek. Looking up, she saw the giant wings of the evil bird circling above. How huge Jijogweh was!

How long was his sharp beak! But quickly she reached for her arrow.

"Aaaaeee!" wailed Brave Girl, staring at the arrow shaft which hung like a wilted blade of grass in her hand. "The wet night air has taken the life from my arrows!"

But the strong young woman would not let herself lose courage. "Good spirits of the night, be my friends!" Brave Girl called, grasping her medicine pouch. Then, as Jijogweh loomed closer, she drew another arrow, whispering the powerful words taught to her by the medicine man. This time her arrow lay firm against her bow. Shooting straight and true, Brave Girl pierced the wicked heart of the blood-thirsty bird.

The monster fell, its wings beating the air wildly and thrashing the water until it foamed. Then as the evil bird sank beneath the surface forever, a flock of gulls rose like a cloud from the water, hovered a moment, and flew away.

The storytellers say that Jijogweh had eaten the gulls in his terrible hunger and they were released at last by his death. Jijogweh's ghost still haunts the clouds but he cannot suck the blood of humans. Now, whenever Jijogweh makes

31

a storm, the gulls fly up to warn the people. It's their way of thanking Brave Girl.

THUNDER AND LIGHTNING

Many Indian tribes have a thunder story. In some, Thunder is a powerful messenger of the Almighty, often in the form of an enormous bird. The Thunderbird of the Assiniboin teaches its children by making a loud noise which they repeat over and over.

The Thompson River Indians have a funny story about Thunder. An envious Thunder noticed that Mosquito was very fat and wondered where he got so much to eat. Mosquito was afraid that if he told the truth, Thunder would eat up all the people. "I suck on trees," Mosquito answered. So today Thunder shoots trees with his bolts of lightning rather than shooting people.

In this story from Puget Sound tribes, Thunder and Lightning were once two brothers who roamed the mountains.

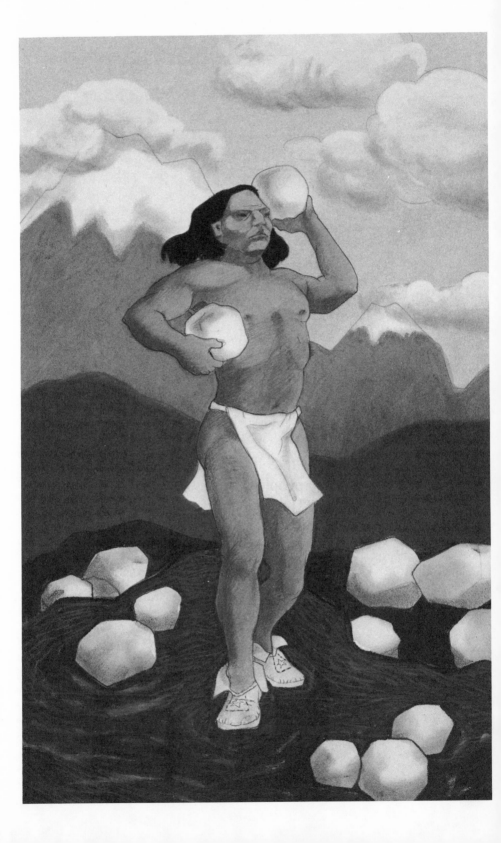

HOW THUNDER
AND LIGHTNING
CAME

ENUMCLAW and Kapoonis were brothers who were fine hunters but wanted to become something more. These two brothers were often away from the village for many moons, hunting wild game, drying the meat, and hiding it to use later. But their travels had another purpose because each searched for a guardian spirit that would make him a great medicine man.

Kapoonis tried to find his guardian spirit in a vision. Every morning and every night he took baths in the river so he might be worthy of a powerful vision. That's how he found a fire spirit so powerful that he was able to throw flames from one bank of the river to the other.

Meanwhile Enumclaw grew strong too. In the mountains he practiced tossing stones from one peak to another, making sharp cracking sounds. Sometimes he threw the stones against rocks to call his younger brother or send him signals. Each day Enumclaw threw larger stones. Each day the cracks grew louder.

When he saw people crossing the mountains, Enumclaw threw rocks at the nearby peaks warning his brother that someone was near. But now the terrible noise hurt the ears of the people and made them run home. "Enumclaw frightens the largest birds and makes them fly so fast their wings make loud rumbles!" cried the people. "And Kapoonis throws arrows of fire from peak to peak!"

Enumclaw and Kapoonis did not know the people were frightened. To them, it was a game to test their power.

One night the two brothers sat on a rocky ridge facing the setting sun. "Look Kapoonis," said his brother. "There is a great white rock across the river. I will throw stones on the left side of the rock so hard that the ridge along the river will fall."

"Sounds like fun!" said Kapoonis. "I'll flash my bolts of fire to the right."

Enumclaw threw his stones as hard as he could and Kapoonis hurled out great bolts of flame, igniting the sky and sending the people to hide and cover their ears. Afterwards, there was nothing left of the ridge along the river.

From above the peaks, the Great Spirit watched the brothers playing their games and wrecking the land. "It is too dangerous for humans to have so much power," said the Great Spirit. So he made Enumclaw and Kapoonis thunder and lightning and gave them a new home far above the people.

RAINBOW

"The Rain's Hat"; "The Great Spirit's Fishing Line"; "Strong-Medicine-to-Drive-Away-Rain"; "Cloud-Boy's Sky Path." These were names given to the rainbow by different tribes across the country. To the Zia, rainbows were paths that only war heroes were allowed to travel. But the Yuchi said the gods had stretched a rainbow across the sky to prevent any more rain from falling.

This story from the Hoh and Quileute tribes is about a mysterious rainbow woman who lived on the other side of the ocean. The Hoh and Quileute live on the Olympic Peninsula in the state of Washington.

THE HUNTER AND RAINBOW WOMAN

ONE FINE morning long ago, a hunter shot a duck with a newly made arrow. The arrow did not harm the duck, but settled deep in her feathers. When she flew away, the arrow flew with her.

To the hunter, this was a very special arrow, so he followed the duck, hoping to get it back. All day he pursued the duck until he was completely lost, but still he went on. He followed the duck to the far side of the ocean. When finally he reached the opposite shore, there was a surprise waiting. The duck had changed into a giant woman!

"Now I have you!" screamed the giant as she snatched the hunter. "I've been waiting to catch a new husband, and here you are!" Grabbing a hank of the hunter's hair, the giantess pulled him along beside her. On their way to her house, they passed a neighbor, who whispered a few words of caution to the hunter.

"Watch out! Tonight she'll kill you and eat you, just like the others!"

Late that night when the hunter thought the giant was asleep, he escaped. He dashed through the trees, over the hills and along the water until once more he was lost. He could hear the giant woman's thundering footsteps in the

39

distance. Suddenly a beautiful woman dressed in cloth of many colors appeared in his path.

Stopping to catch his breath, the hunter asked, "Who are you?"

"I am Rainbow Woman," said the stranger. "Why are you running so fast?"

"Don't you feel the earth tremble?" said the hunter. "Those are the footsteps of an evil giant who wants to kill me."

"Then I can help you," replied Rainbow Woman. "Run on ahead. I'll follow in a moment."

When Rainbow Woman caught up with the hunter, they could hear the giant woman thumping down the path, shaking all the trees as she rumbled along. Then, WOOMP! and everything was silent.

"What did you do?" asked the hunter.

"I set a trap," said Rainbow Woman. "Now, come along and rest at my house," she said, for already she loved him.

So the hunter went off with the beautiful Rainbow Woman and by morning he had fallen in love too.

The hunter married Rainbow Woman and after a while, they had a child. But one morning the hunter took his bow and arrows, as he often did, and went hunting. When he had not returned by afternoon, Rainbow Woman went out to look for him, but she could not find him. To this day, he has not returned.

Rainbow Woman knows her husband has just lost his way again, so she keeps watch faithfully. Sometimes she climbs into the sky so she can see better to search the land. When we see a double rainbow, we know her child is searching with her, too.

WHERE THE TALES
BEGAN

1. **EARTH IS ON BIG TURTLE'S BACK** was recorded in 1899 by William E. Connelley who was adopted by Wyandots of the Deer Clan and given the name, Rainbow.

2. **THIRSTY LIZARD ENDS THE BIG FLOOD** was included in a collection of legends about the Pikes Peak area by Ernest Whitney in 1892.

3. **DAYLIGHT COMES AT LAST** is part of a longer tale told in 1912 by James A. Teit for the *Journal of American Folklore*.

4. **BIG ELK DIGS UP THE MOUNTAINS** was told by Laforia, a very old Jicarilla Apache woman, whose grandson, Gunsi, interpreted it for Frank Russell in 1898.

5. **THE MAKING OF WHIRLWIND** was inspired in part by a Kiowa tale, briefly recorded by Elsie Clews Parsons in 1929, which was told by Old Man Slim, who received both the story and his name from his mother's grandfather.

6. **BRAVE GIRL AND THE STORM MONSTER** is one of many Iroquois legends written by Harriet Maxwell Converse in 1908.

7. **HOW THUNDER AND LIGHTNING CAME** was told by Henry Sicade to Hermann Haeberlin and published in the *Tacoma Evening News* in 1916.

8. **THE HUNTER AND RAINBOW WOMAN**, told by Klekabuk, was recorded some time between 1905 and 1909 by Albert B. Reagan while he was a government agent for the Hoh and Quileute tribes.

GLOSSARY

Appalachian Mountains–the major mountain system in eastern United States, extending from Canada to Alabama

Avalanche–a mass of snow, ice, or earth falling down a mountain side

Beaver–a large rodent with a broad, flat tail. With its long front teeth, the beaver cuts trees and uses them to build dams and dens along streams

Black spider–a web-spinning arachnid

Blizzard–a violent snowstorm with high winds

Buffalo–North American bison

Camas root–the edible bulb of the camas plant, a member of the lily family

Canoe–a long, narrow boat made of wood, bark or hides. Canoes made from birchbark were lightweight and easy for one or a few to carry. Some dugout canoes, made from huge logs, could carry more than fifty people.

Cascade Range–a chain of forested mountains in western United States extending from British Columbia to Northern California

Chips–small pieces of wood or dried buffalo dung used for fuel

Coal–a black mineral which burns and is used for fuel

Council–a group of leaders who make decisions for the tribe

Coyote–a swift, cunning mammal, related to, but smaller than, the wolf

Cyclone–a storm with high winds circulating around a center of low pressure

Down–soft, fine feathers

Duck–a waterfowl with a flat bill and webbed feet

Eagle–a large, powerful bird of prey with sharp vision

Earthquake–shaking of the earth's surface, usually caused by movement of underground rock.

Elders–the older people of a tribe

Elk–the largest member of the deer family. Older males have large antlers with many tines.

Ember–a smoldering piece of wood or coal

Fog–a fine mist or cloud near the ground

Gopher–a brownish burrowing rodent with large front teeth and long front claws

Guardian Spirit–a supernatural being that was a personal spiritual helper and the source of a man's or a woman's power

Gull–a web-footed water bird found near all oceans and many lakes

Iroquois Confederacy–a league of five Native American nations including Mohawk, Oneida, Onondaga, Cayuga and Seneca, and joined later by the Tuscaroras

Hailstones–pellets of frozen rain

Hawthorne–a shrub or small tree with long thorns

Herb–a plant used as medicine or flavoring

Heron–a large wading bird with long legs and broad wings

Hickory–a tree of the walnut family with hard, tough wood

Leech–a segmented worm which usually feeds on blood. Most live in water.

Lizard–a long-tailed, four-legged reptile, most commonly found in warm climates

Loon–a diving water bird with a laughing call

Marsh–swampy, wet land

Medicine Man–a tribe member said to have supernatural healing powers

Mississippi River–large river of central United States, flowing south from Northern Minnesota to the Gulf of Mexico

Moccasins–soft, leather slippers

Mosquito–a small insect with long legs. The female feeds on the blood of animals.

Muskrat–a brown rodent found in ponds, streams and marshes

Northwest Coast–an area of the North American Pacific Coast extending northward from Northern California to Alaska

Northern Lights–the aurora borealis. Luminous forms of color in the night sky.

Otter–a water mammal of the weasel family with a slender body and thick, brown fur

Pikes Peak–a 14,100-foot mountain in the front range of the Rocky Mountains in Colorado

Pitch–resin found in evergreen trees

Plain–an expanse of level land

Poplar–a deciduous tree of the willow family having lightweight, soft wood

Puget Sound–a huge bay between the Olympic Peninsula and the Cascade Mountains in Washington State

Rabbit–a small, short-tailed mammal common in North America, with hind legs adapted to running and jumping

Rainbow–an arc of colors of the spectrum appearing in the sky when sunlight shines through rain or mist

Raven–a glossy black bird of the crow family with a croaking call

Salmon–a fish. The Pacific Salmon is known for the long journeys it makes upstream to its breeding grounds.

Serpent–a snake

Sinew–dried fibers of an animal tendon

Sleet–partly frozen rain or a mixture of rain and snow

Smoke hole–an opening in the lodge or structure through which smoke escapes

Smoking spear–a gun

Sucker fish–a freshwater fish with a mouth adapted for sucking

Swan–a large water bird with a long, slender neck

Thermal waters–water which is warmer than the surrounding air and which flows or spouts from deep in the ground where rocks are hot

Thong–a narrow strip of leather

Toad–an amphibian similar to the frog, generally found in moist places

Tornado–a dark, destructive, funnel-shaped cloud with violent rotating air, extending from a cloud mass to the earth

Tunnel–an underground passage

Turtle–a reptile with a hard shell covering a soft body

Volcano–a vent on the earth's surface through which lava, gases and rocks are discharged from below. A cone-shaped mountain of these materials may form around the vent.

Warrior–a person experienced in fighting wars

Whirlwind–a violently revolving current of forward-moving air

Wolf–a flesh-eating mammal related to the dog

SOURCES OF INFORMATION

Wm. N. Byers, INDIAN LEGENDS, Out West Magazine, July, 1873; Wm. N. Canfield, THE LEGENDS OF THE IROQUOIS, 1902, reprint by Ira Friedman, 1971; Harriet Maxwell Converse, MYTHS AND LEGENDS OF THE NEW YORK IROQUOIS, Education Department Bulletin #437, Dec. 15, 1908, University of the State of New York; Ellen Russell Emerson, INDIAN MYTHS, Boston, 1884; James Athearn Jones, TALES OF AN INDIAN CAMP, London, 1830; Walter McClintock, THE OLD NORTH TRAIL, London, 1910; Marion Foster Washburne, INDIAN LEGENDS, Rand McNally and Co., Chicago, 1915; Ernest Whitney, M.A., LEGENDS OF THE PIKES PEAK REGION, Denver, 1892; Theodore Winthrop, THE CANOE AND SADDLE, Boston, 1893; Reports from the Bureau of American Ethnology, Volumes 14, 19, and 31; Journal of American Folklore, Volumes 11, 12, 13, 25, 37, and 46; University of California Publications in American Archaeology, Volume 4; Colorado Historical Society, Denver; Milwaukee County Public Museum.

Very special thanks are due Dr. Alice B. Kehoe, anthropologist and author of NORTH AMERICAN INDIANS: A COMPREHENSIVE ACCOUNT, and Judy Turner of the Milwaukee County Public Museum library.